ORGANIZE THAT MESS!

Written By: Tonia Monroe

ISBN: 979-8-845-97572-0

Headshot Photo Credit: Kenneth Grant Inzpiration

This book is dedicated to you for taking the time to better your day-to-day by getting organized. Today is the day you decided to get focused, opting to operate wisely and effectively, getting out of the mess!

Here are a few words of encouragement to get you started with a positive and productive mindset.

"You don't have to stop everything to get organized. You just have to start." – Donna Smallin

"For every minute spent organizing, an hour is earned." – Benjamin Franklin

"Organizing is a journey, not a destination." – Unknown

"Strive not to get more done, but to have less to do." – Francine Jay

Table of Contents

Introduction

You have goals, plans, and aspirations. However, you can't seem to focus on them. Is it because you can't remember what they are? Maybe you have too many distractions. Whatever the reasons are now is the time to get serious, starting with clearing out physical and mental space. This book is intended to help you do just that!

Inside, you will find tips, advice, and tool suggestions to get you organized, and on your path towards progress and success.

The main topics we're going to focus on are:

- Career based organizing
- Education based organizing
- Home based organizing

You are worthy of clarity!

The purpose of this book is to get you straight! Through the pages, you will receive a variety of tips to help with your day-to-day, with occasional reality checks along the way.

Where did this passion for neatness come from? I became a neat freak by default. I was raised around family members who were hoarders, and it triggered an impulse to sort things into their proper place. It drove me nuts seeing mail, clothes, toys, etc. everywhere. I began breaking the cycle early.

        While I have some experience with personal organizing for individuals, my preference lies in a more professional setting. Assisting students and business professionals get their lives sorted with their items is helping them towards the path of success. And assisting people to strive towards becoming successful is one of the greatest gifts I've ever given myself.

        We're all meant to have some form of an organized lifestyle. Now it's up to you to find out what works and stick to it. That's where I come in!

Note: Read through each tip as they may be helpful in areas other than their designated chapters. Each tip and suggestion may spark different ideas for you!

OFFICE

"Good order is the foundation of all things." – Edmund Burke

Paperclips

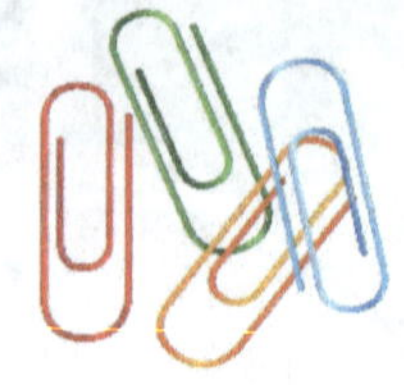

Not to get confused with binder clips, I want to talk about some great purposes for paperclips, as pictured above. My favorite and most commonly used methods for benefiting from paperclips are:

- As a bookmark. Because of the tight grip, I never have to worry about the clip falling off, causing me to lose my place. One down side will be the temporary dent that may be left on a few pages.
- For sorting documents. Group related documents together that are related, but not related enough to be bound by a staple. For example, two documents related to the same client, but one is specific to their business, while the other is regarding their personal history.
- To indicate priority. Why stick to only using the standard silver clips? Switch it up by placing red on important or rush paperwork, and softer toned colors on things that can wait.

Sticky Notes

I have a confession: I *LOVE* sticky notes! I value this tool because of its variety. They come in so many shapes, sizes, colors, and even textures, that the possibilities become endless. Here's a breakdown to give you an idea on uses that fit your needs:

- Bold colors = Reminders and attention grabbers for documents, or items around your desk (such as on your keys to remind you to grab your lunch bag before you leave).
- Size 4"x6" and up = Quick notes
- Arrow shapes, any size = Labels for drawers, cords, binders, folders, etc. These are also great for turning them into tabs or flags, separating documents into easy to find sections.
- Transparent, and color = for labeling.
- Any size, shape, color, or texture = as a bookmark.

*TIP: Did you know that there is a way to remove a single sticky note from its pad, without it curling up? The key is to remove it from side to side. Lifting from a bottom corner to the top creates a bend, which makes the paper curl.

Can you think of more benefits? Share with your fellow organizers by joining our social media groups!

Planner

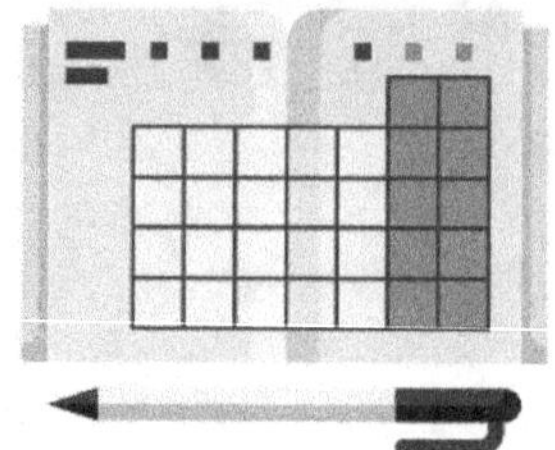

- ☐ Don't have space for a large calendar?
- ☐ Use a calendar, but don't want folks in your business?
- ☐ Forget to update your electronic calendar because it's out of sight and out of mind?
- ☐ Tired of not having enough space to write on your calendar?

If you answered yes to at least one of these questions, it's time to get a planner! I'll be honest and admit that all four have been a yes for me at one point or another. Now, while I am a huge advocate for planners, you can end up buying the wrong type. To help you make the best judgment call, consider the following:

What are you using the planner for?

- Keeping track of finances: Consider a financial planner. They typically come with sections to help you budget and track bills and financial goals.
- Keeping track of health: Consider a fitness planner. These typically come with sections to help you with meal prepping and tracking your health progress.
- Staying on top of tasks: Consider a to-do list-based planner. It'll help you feel productive as you check items off of your list, as long as you give yourself realistic goals to accomplish.
- Multi-use or unknown/undecided: Consider either a bullet journal, or a traditional daily/weekly planner.

For specific tips based on the four questions asked at the start of this section, I've come up with these:

Don't have space for a large calendar?

Feel free to utilize whichever planner suits your needs, as they're all typically travel sized. The largest planner I've come across could still fit in my laptop bag.

Use a calendar, but don't want folks in your business?

With a planner, your privacy is completely up to you. If you're going to walk away from your planner while it's open, it's just as in the open as posting up a huge calendar. Personally, I also take mine home after a day in the office. Even if I don't have my personal business in my planner, I may have jotted down a client's phone number or email address, and I value their privacy too much to leave it unattended.

Forget to update your electronic calendar because it's out of sight and out of mind?

Keep your planner in front of where you sit. You can prop it against your monitor, right above your keyboard, etc. If this doesn't work, place it in your snack drawer! Worst case, decorate it in a way it stands out with bold colors, sparkles, stickers, or all three.

Tired of not having enough space to write on your calendar?

I recommend a daily planner for the most space, as they offer one or two full pages to write on for each day. Is this a little too much space? A weekly planner may be a better for you.

*TIP: Worried about losing your page? Most planners come with a bookmark!

Mason Jars

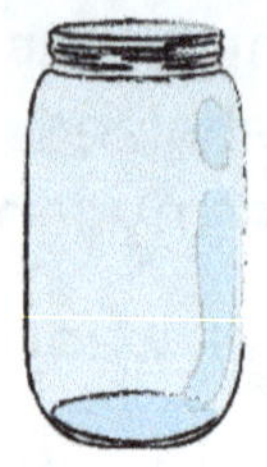

Because mason jars are transparent, I love having them to sort and store items such as:

- Push pins
- Paperclips
- Spare staples
- Pens and pencils
- Rulers
- Ideas (as an idea jar)
- Erasers
- Spare tape rolls
- Sticky notes
- Spare eating utensils

Mason jars will keep those pesky loose items in a designated area, easy to locate and grab when needed. Basically, this tool is for small and loose stationery items. Try to limit yourself to about 3 jars, unless you have a safe way to stack or store them. If you have more items than what can fit and be sorted into 3 jars, a desk caddy will be a much better tool for you.

Career Specific Tips

Teacher/Professor/Education Worker

- Color code storage bins, binders, etc.
- Opt for in-sight storage
- Utilize decorative push pins

Desk/Cubicle/Station Worker

- Opt for out-of-sight storage
- Utilize cord and office supply organizers and caddies
- Less is more. Don't get lost by having too much in your line of vision.

Hands-On/Warehouse Worker

- Utilize pocket sized tools, such as a pen, highlighter, small notepad, sticky notes, and binder/paper clips.

If your profession type/style is not listed, it may be because I am not familiar with the day-to-day workflow. However, I'm open to learn more, so feel free to tell me about your profession by emailing info@toniamonroe.com.

SCHOOL

"Organization begins with awareness of what doesn't work for us." – FillingTheJars.com

Highlighter

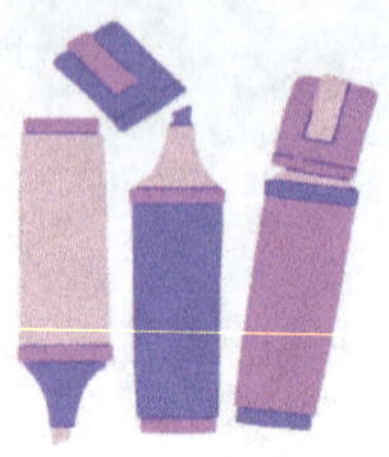

In case you are unfamiliar, or have never used a highlighter, welcome to color, my friend! Basically, highlighters are semi-transparent markers. Using highlighters, both physical and digital, help make information stand out. They come in a wide variety of colors, shapes, and sizes to fit your needs.

To best benefit your uses of highlighters, use a color code. This will help you keep focused, and avoid going color crazy. An example of what my color code may look like on a document is:

- Yellow – Important, add to notes
- Blue – Ask about this, I'm confused
- Pink – Add to presentation as refresher for team

In an office setting, you may find that highlighters play a big role during presentations.

Now, let's jump into the benefits for you as a student:

- Saves valuable time (pinpoint important details/summary)
- Determines the important parts (avoid unnecessary info)
- Improves the quality of your notes (points out great study notes)
- Helps you remember (make important keywords/phrases stand out)

*TIP: If you've highlighted more than 1/3 of the page, you've done too much! Your textbook is not a coloring book; keep it simple.

*Tip: If you intend on making copies of your document, only use yellow, orange, or pink highlighters. Any other color will appear too dark, making it difficult to read. Yellow won't show through at all, and orange and pink will show very lightly.

Pen

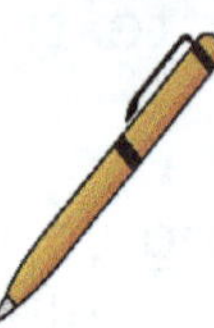

We're all familiar with what pens are and how to use them. So, instead of me breaking down its uses, here's a list of tips to assist you with maximizing the benefits:

- Stay away from ink that bleeds through paper. It will make your notes difficult to read, and likely smear into an inky mess.
- Ballpoint pens are best for gliding across a page. These are especially helpful for folks like myself who write in cursive, not picking up the pen between letters.
- Utilize multiple colors to separate class subjects. If you're using one notebook or planner for all of your courses, keep them separate and easy to identify by giving each course its own color.

- If you intend on making copies or your notes or document, only use dark colored inks like dark blue or black. Red is another color that will show up when copied, but it also makes your original document look unprofessional. Colors like light blue, green, pink and orange will be hard to read, or may not be visible at all. I learned this lesson the hard way!

Planner

If you're thinking to yourself "I don't need a planner," stop lying, get a planner, and let's get to work! Now that we've cleared that up, I'm going to explain the benefits of using a planner, as well as methods to maximize its effectiveness.

Benefits:

- Keep track of due dates
- Keep track of tests, exams, and finals
- Keep track of projects and group members
- Keep track of courses
    - Course ID
    - Professor contact information

Methods:

- Plan in advance. When you receive your course syllabus, instead of writing the assignment due dates on their actual due dates, write them in your planner a week in advance. Why?
    - ☐ You are less likely to submit assignments late.
    - ☐ It will cover you in the chance an emergency pops up. The tasks for that week have already been completed. Just catch up when you return!
- Color code courses. If you have 3 or more courses, help yourself keep them sorted in your planner by designating each one its own color.
- Simply put, use it! Get into the habit of not only writing in your planner, but of also reading what you

wrote. Pick a couple of days of the week as "review planner" days to start off until you've gotten accustomed to your new best friend.

Index Cards

We may all be familiar with flash cards, but is this all you've ever used index cards for? This tool can be for taking quick notes, easily sort-able by course subjects. Index cards helped me to prioritize my study notes. I would only write down the information that I couldn't remember. One of my college professors (Dr. Trey) would let us use one index card full of notes to help with our tests. Because the average card is so small (about 4" x 6"), I really had to make the most of the space available.

In a more professional setting, index cards are also good for:

- Maintaining client information. Store the cards on a Rolodex or in a box.
- Taking quick notes during meetings. These can be sorted by projects.
- Presentation notes. Write down key focus points.

*TIP: Write in color to help you visually remember your notes. Adding stickers or drawings that relate to the study topic can also assist.

*TIP: For storage, hole punch a corner in each card, and place them all on a binder ring. You can also place them inside of an index card, often equipped with divider tabs and labels.

Learning Style Tools and Tips

Visual Learner

Colorful pens, highlighters, stickers and sticky notes will help you identify and remember topics by pairing them with a color. When it's a serious topic or something extremely important to remember, color it red or any other color that makes you think it's a priority. If the study topic made you laugh or smile, color those notes in your favorite color. Don't be afraid to get creative!

Auditory Learner

Try utilizing a tape recorder or voice recording app. While you're in class, you can listen in depth to the lesson. Then when you're home, you can play the lesson back to take notes with. Not only will this allow you to catch details you may have missed the first time, but it will help you pick up on your pitch changes in your instructor's voice that will help you remember what was taught during testing time.

Hands-On Learner

The top tools that will come handy for you are index cards and paper. Write down your notes twice. First as an extended version on regular paper, then write a summarized, quick study version on index cards. You may be surprised at how much you could remember writing!

See page 36 for study tips based on each learning style. View the downloadable version by visiting www.ToniaMonroe.com.

HOME

"If you've had something for six months and it's still not repaired, it's clutter." – Gretch Rubin

Kitchen

For many families, this room is the heart of their home. In the kitchen is where we come to get our daily nutrition. Because of its importance, why not make sure that it is being operated at its maxed efficiency? Try these tools around your kitchen to help everyone who enters it.

Index Cards	Grocery Lists
Index Cards	Recipes (store in a box or on a ring)
Paperclip	Sealing bags (cereal, snacks)
Mason Jars	Storing dry goods (beans, pasta, rice) – Must have an airtight lid
Clear Containers	Storing dry goods (beans, pasta, rice) – Must have an airtight lid
Desk Caddy	Sorting small items (sauce packages, individually wrapped snacks, cooking utensils, etc.)
Can Rack	Sorting canned goods, and organizing baby bottles
Mason Jars	Storing small items (toothpicks, paperclips, etc.)
Tape	Use for labeling
Notepads	Grocery Lists
Magnet	Prioritize important reminders by sticking them to the fridge (don't go crazy). For example: take steak out of the freezer, or

	"good by (DATE)" charts for perishable items.
Magnet Strip	Sorting metal cooking utensils
Magnet Strip	Sorting mason jars

Office

    This space can be more difficult to keep neat than a company office because of all of the other surrounding rooms, and you don't have peers judging your desk. It is important to keep the items belonging to other rooms in the house, out of the office. As a "snacker", I struggle with keeping food out. However, by remembering to only bring office tools into the office, it forces me to get out of that room every now and then, and stretch my legs. Now, for the items that *belong* in the office, here are some tools to help you store them:

Mason Jar	Pen/marker holder
Mason Jar	Storing small items (staples, erasers, paperclips, push pins, etc.)
Desk Caddy	Alternative to using mason jars
Paperclips	Page marker to pinpoint information
Sticky Notes	Quick note taking
Sticky Notes	Pops of color for inspiration and reminders
Index Cards	Storing notes or client information (store in box or on a ring)
Tape	Use for labeling
Sticky Notes	Use for labeling
Note Pads	Quick note taking
Magnet	Useful for storing reminders on metal filing cabinets

Magnet Strip	Sorting mason jars, loose paperclips, push pins, letter openers, scissors, etc.
Can Rack	Alternative option for storing mason jars
Calendar	Keep your eyes on your tasks and goals

Kid's Room

This room can be tricky, so I suggest you utilize all four corners of the room, and give each corner its own purpose.

- o Play Corner – Toys/Games
- o Sleeping Corner – Bed/Bedding
- o Clothing Corner – Closet/Dresser/Accessories
- o Learning Corner – Bookshelf/Desk/Reading Nook

Play Corner

- Should contain all items purchased in the toy department: dolls/action figures, noise makers, things that light up
- This corner is for sparking creativity and having fun

Sleeping Corner

- Should contain only the items necessary for peaceful sleep: bed and accessories, night light, stuffed toy (if preferred)

Clothing Corner

- Should only contain body accessories: clothes, shoes, socks, head accessories, etc.

Learning Corner

- Should contain items such as a comfy chair, books, and a desk/table
- This corner is for stimulating the mind and relaxing

Master Bedroom

The bedroom tends to become messy because it's often used as a common area. Stop doing that! Keep food in the kitchen, toys in the play area, clothes in the closet, and electronics in the office area.

*TIP: Store clothing from head to toe. Hats and head wraps on top, clothes in the middle, and shoes at the bottom.

*TIP: If your bed frame provides space between the bed and the floor, utilize that space for storage. Purchasing storage bins, or creating your own storage unit, will help you free up space in your room. I suggest you store items under the bed that you don't use often. Just make sure it belongs in the bedroom! Exception, as not every home offers a linen closet and spare bathroom pantry: toiletries and linen. Disclaimer: If you have a bed frame with mechanics, such as the ability to vibrate and lift the mattress, I don't recommend storing flammable items under the bed for obvious fire hazard reasons.

Garage/Shed

Alright, let's be honest. A garage and shed are both areas that often get packed and forgotten about.

- × If you cannot walk through this space without bumping into something, you have too much.
- × If you cannot see the floor, you have too much.
- × If you cannot fit your vehicle in the garage, you have too much.

What do you use this space for?

- Storing collectibles and supplies? Store items in labeled filing containers and bins. If out of sight, out of mind means you'll forget where things are (even with the labels), opt for transparent bins.
- Storing tools? Keep everything visible, utilizing racks, shelves, and magnet strips.

Here's a breakdown of helpful tool suggestions to keep your storage space neat:

Magnet Strip	Sorting items containing metal (tools, jars, etc.)
Mason Jar	Storing small items (nails, screws, staples, glue sticks, etc.)
Sticky Note	Labeling
Tape	Labeling
Sticky Note	Quick notes

Tool Tower	Storing large tools (shovels, wrapping paper, etc.)
Can Rack	Storing jars
Wall Calendar	Keep track of goals and to-do lists for the week. A dry-erase, chalk, or corkboard will also suffice.

<u>*Introduction to available info products*</u>

Goal Setting Chart

Study Guide

Accountability Chart

Additional products to come!

If you have any suggestions, or products that will better help you, let me know at info@toniamonroe.com. We can work on tailoring something just for you.

Goal Setting Chart

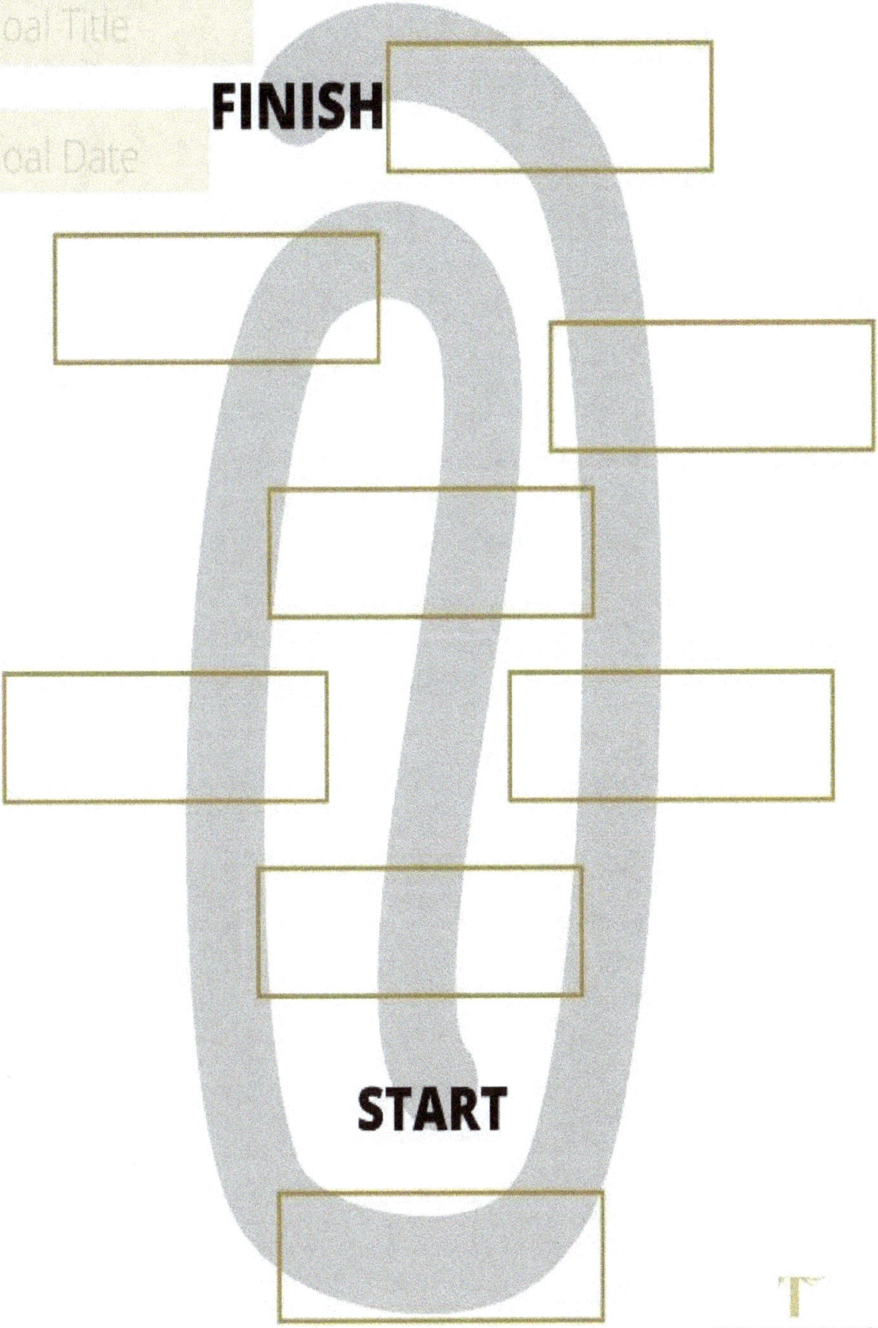

Goal Setting Chart

Goal Title

Goal Date

FINISH

START

Goal Setting Chart

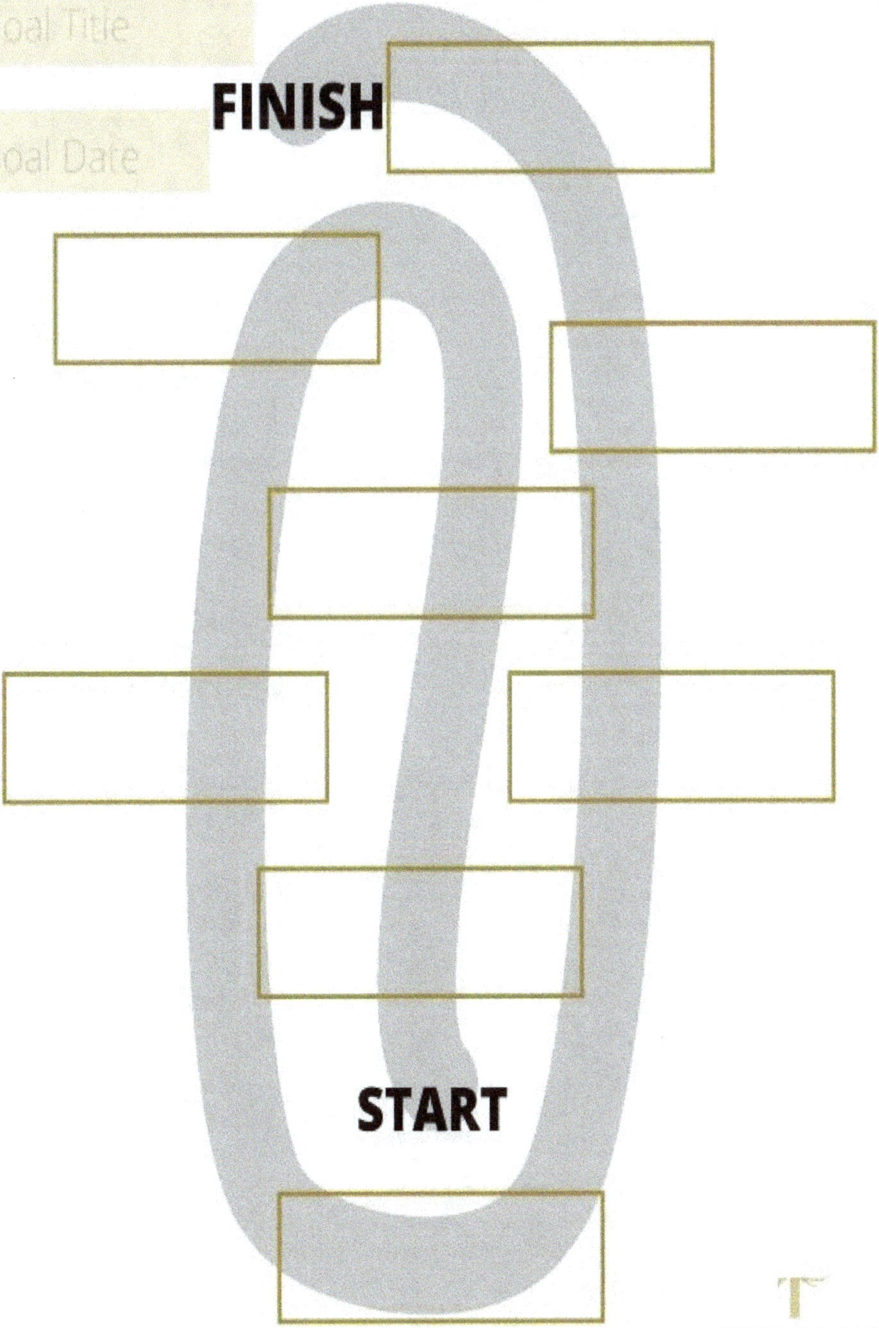

Goal Setting Chart

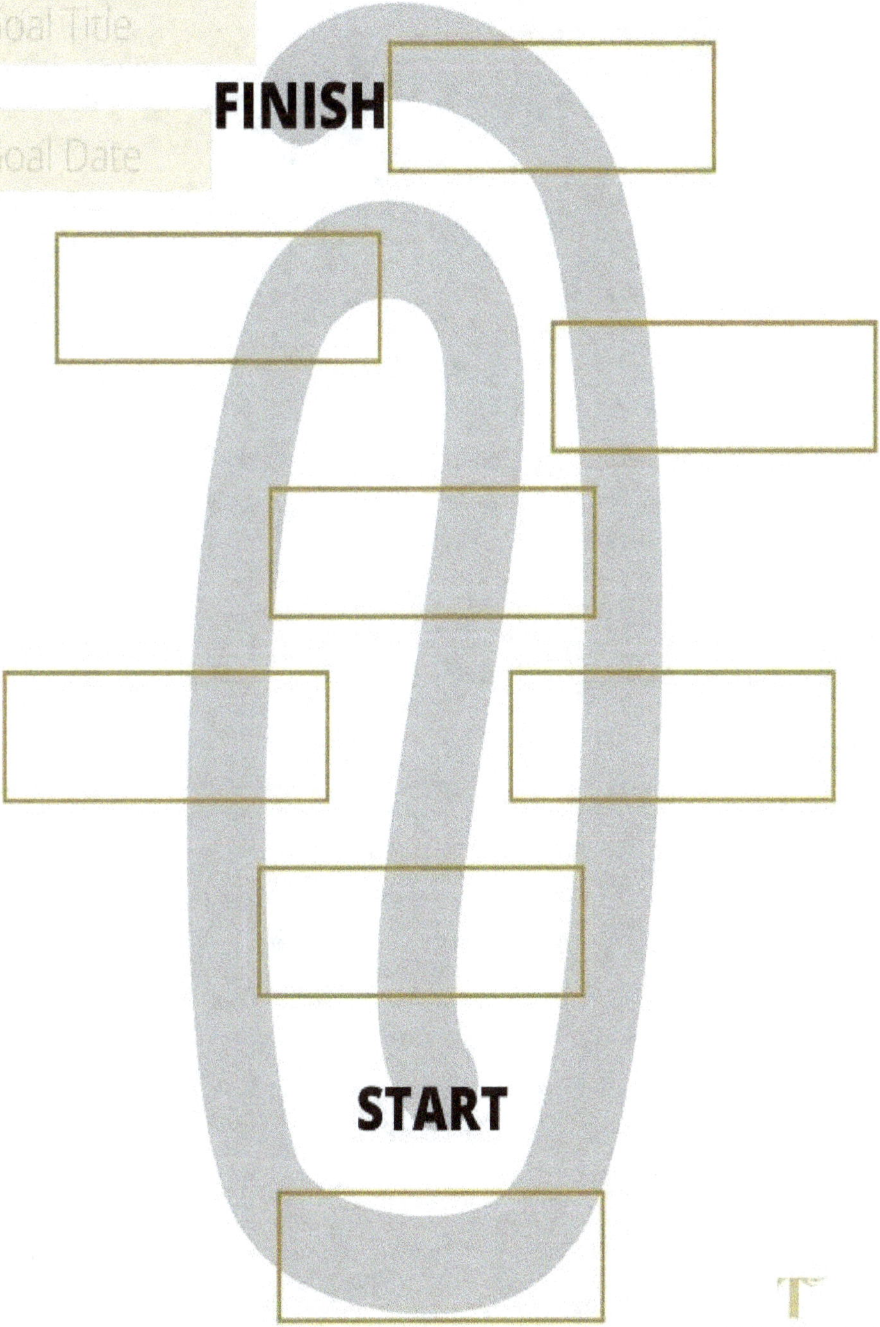

Goal Setting Chart

Goal Title

Goal Date

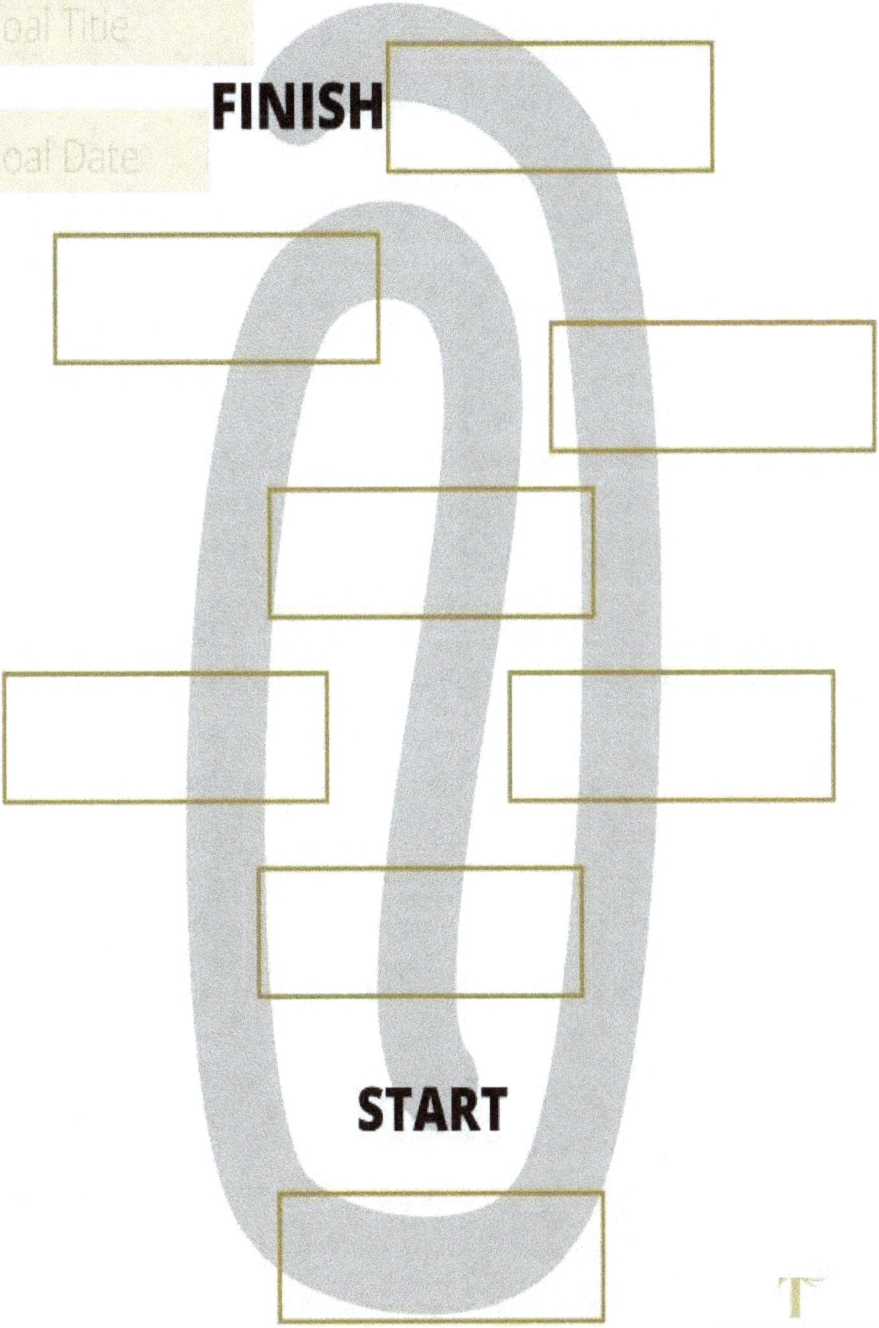

FINISH

START

TONIA MONROE

BASIC STUDY GUIDE FOR EACH LEARNING STYLE

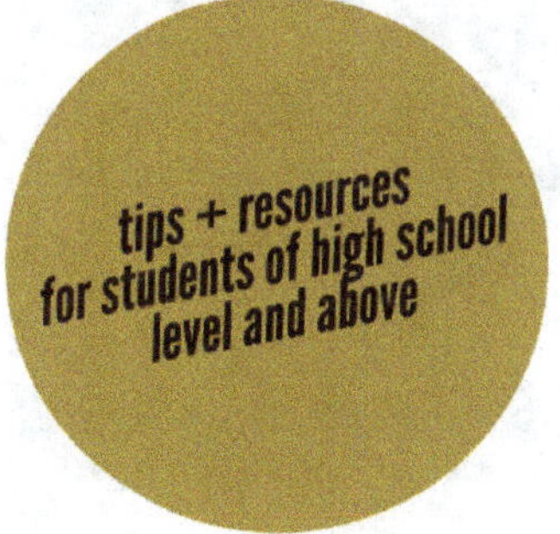

VISUAL LEARNER

INCORPORATE COLORS

It's important to utilize colors to help topics stand out. When you designate subjects with their own color, it becomes easier to remember what you've read. Products such as pens and highlighters will be your best friend!

UTILIZE STICKY NOTES

Sticky notes have multiple uses that can benefit your studying, such as:

- Making pop-up notes
- Bookmarking sections
- Adding removable color

POSITION MATTERS

Organize your study space to create the ultimate learning environment. Place important reminders or key study points at eye level, to give yourself important objects to look at if you find yourself wandering.

RE-WRITE NOTES

Give yourself the option to see your notes again. Often times, when you can see notes written in a familiar handwriting (yours!), it makes it easier for the brain to recall what was written.

UTLIZE FLASH CARDS

Flash/index cards provide a smaller space to dedicate individual focus on topics. It allows just enough space to add a subject, and a brief description or story. This will help maintain focus on specific details.

INCORPORATE DIAGRAMS & ILLUSTRATIONS

Add stickers, graphs, or drawings related to your study topic into your notes. It'll help you remember details of a noun when you can actually see them!

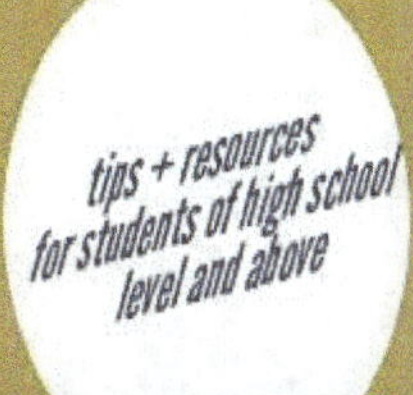

AUDITORY LEARNER

RECORD LESSONS

It's always best to hear something twice. Best method is to listen once without taking notes, and listen a second time while taking notes. Record your instructor's lesson (with permission of course), to have their exact wording repeated to you uninterrupted.

READ NOTES OUT LOUD

Because some individuals have a monotone speaking voice, it may be difficult to understand the topic from time to time. Try reading your notes on the subject out loud, and give it personality to help you remember.

TALK ABOUT IT

Present your study topics as if you were the teacher, or discuss them with another classmate. The conversation will assist you in remembering what was talked about, rather than forcing you to only remember what you've read.

SURROUND YOURSELF WITH SILENCE

Block out distracting noises while studying. This will help you focus on what's important, and not on what's the latest gossip on TV shows.

CLOSE YOUR EYES

Enhance your hearing sense by blocking out your visual sense. Keep your mental focused on what you hear versus what you see. Listen to your teacher, instead of focusing on the hair sticking out of their ears!

CREATE MUSIC & RHYMES

Music plays an important role in memory! Have your parents ever asked you "How can you remember these songs, and not your vocabulary words?" Use music to your advantage.

HANDS-ON LEARNER

TAKE BREAKS

Because most course are geared towards visual and auditory learners, it can be difficult for you to focus. Take a break! Walk around, stand up, or grab a snack, and then come back with a fresh mindset.

CREATE A TO-DO LIST

Having the ability to cross items off your list will not only keep you motivated to complete what's on your list, but it will also give your brain a break from reading. Take a moment to grab that pen with smooth glide, and check off the latest chapter.

INCORPORATE MOVEMENTS

Being a hands-on learner will require some hands-on studying. Incorporate a dance move or exercise into your studies to eliminate the constant fidgeting you may have started, and reclaim your focus!

ROLE-PLAY

Act out what you've read with family and friends (or study buddy). The laughs alone should assist with remembering the details, as well as help you feel apart of the action. Be that pirate from the story, peg leg and all.

TAKE WRITTEN NOTES

If viewing notes in your own handwriting doesn't assist you, this will at least keep your hands busy, and your mental focused on what the lesson is. Give it a try, and see if it makes a difference for you.

STUDY OUTDOORS

Put yourself in an environment of peace and fresh air. Clear your mind from stress, close your eyes to the typical routine, and block out the noises of indoor activities. Find clarity so you can focus.

ACCOUNTABILITY CHART

GOAL:

DATE:

DO THESE ASAP

THESE CAN WAIT

MON TUE WED THU FRI SAT SUN

TONIA MONROE

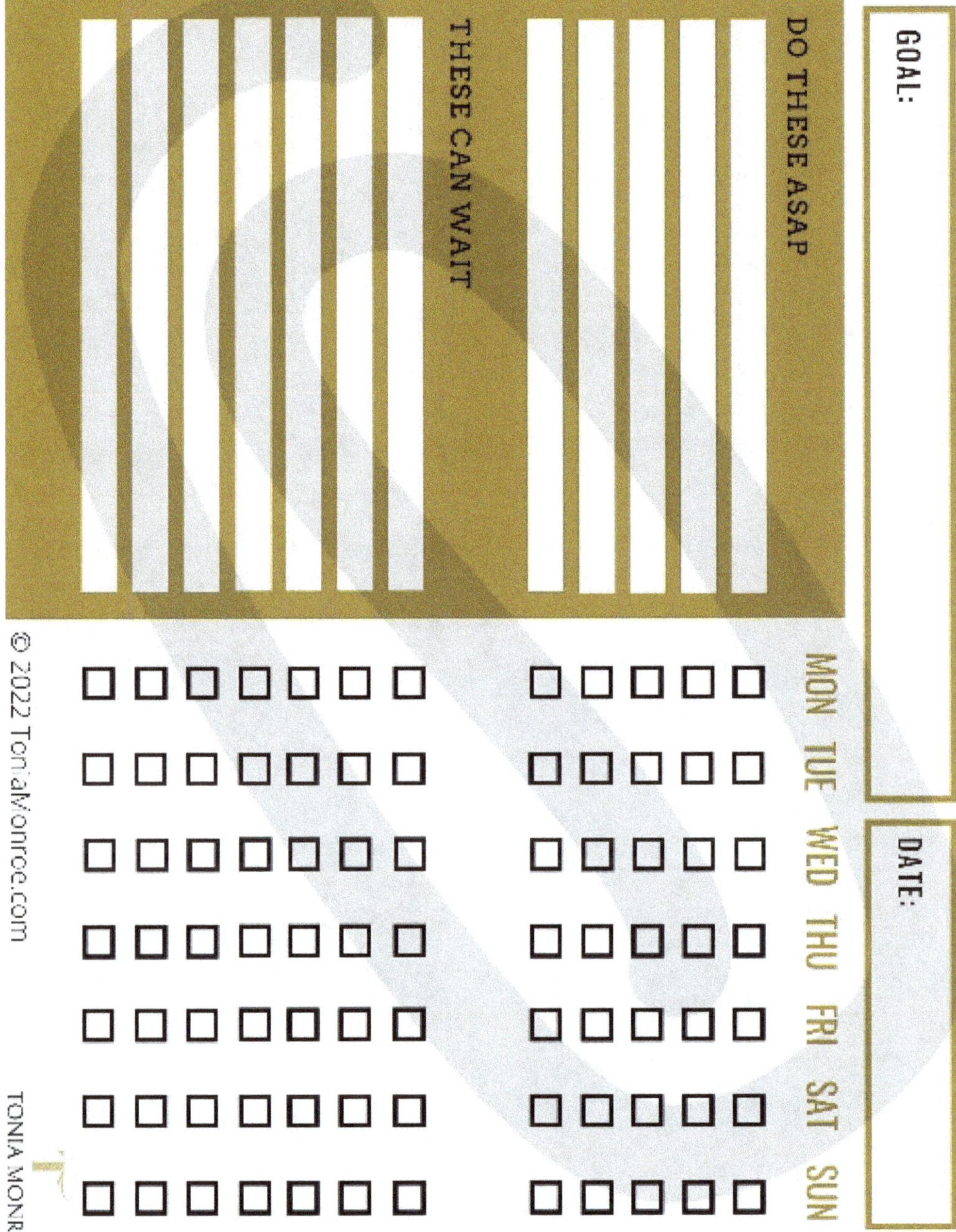

ACCOUNTABILITY CHART
GOAL:
DATE:
DO THESE ASAP
THESE CAN WAIT
MON TUE WED THU FRI SAT SUN
© 2022 ToniaMonroe.com
TONIA MONROE

ACCOUNTABILITY CHART

GOAL:

DATE:

DO THESE ASAP

THESE CAN WAIT

MON TUE WED THU FRI SAT SUN

TONIA MONROE

ACCOUNTABILITY CHART

GOAL:

DATE:

DO THESE ASAP

THESE CAN WAIT

MON TUE WED THU FRI SAT SUN

TONIA MONROE

ACCOUNTABILITY CHART

GOAL:

DATE:

MON TUE WED THU FRI SAT SUN

DO THESE ASAP

THESE CAN WAIT

Notes

Have any of the tips and tools sparked creativity and additional ideas? Jot them down here to have a place to reference!

Notes

Notes

Notes

Be of the first to know about new products and services by visiting ToniaMonroe.com, and joining the email subscription group.

"Tonia was such an awesome addition to Learical Jonez Entertainment Group! She stepped in and organized things that I didn't know needed organizing. There was nothing that I asked her to do that she did not complete. Forever grateful for Tonia joining the team and keeping my scatterbrain organized! Whenever I need something done...and done right? Tonia is my go to...ALWAYS."

Learical J, LJEG CEO

Organize
Your Chaos

STEP 1
Visit www.toniamonroe.com to view our list of services and products.

STEP 2
Book your discovery call to determine where focus should be placed specifically for you.

STEP 3
Utilize the tools and tricks provided by your organization expert.

STEP 4
Exhale! You're out of the chaos!

For inquiries, please visit www.toniamonroe.com, or email info@toniamonroe.com.

<u>*Full List of Tips*</u>

Environment Versus Color

- ☐ Are you in need of energy boosts? Try adding orange to your surroundings.
- ☐ Do you find yourself frequently snacking, and want to stop? Try removing red items from your visual, as the color red promotes hunger.
- ☐ Green is the color of positivity. Add some in your space to help boost the positivity of yourself and those around you.
- ☐ Incorporating shades of purple in your line of vision may help reduce anxiety, blood pressure, and heart rate.

Highlighter

- ☐ If you intend on making copies of your document, only use yellow, orange, or pink highlighters. Any other color will appear too dark, making it difficult to read.
- ☐ If you've highlighted more than 1/3 of the page, you've done too much! Your textbook is not a coloring book; keep it simple.

Home

- ☐ Book bins are great to store tall kitchen utensils and items such as aluminum foil and plastic wrap.
- ☐ If your bed frame provides space between the bed and the floor, utilize that space for storage.
- ☐ LED stick-on lights make a great option over multiple lamps that can clutter your walkway and coffee table.
- ☐ Pack items you don't often use in a box. If you don't find yourself looking for anything in that box within a year, donate everything in it.

- ☐ Store clothing from head to toe. Hats and head wraps on top, clothes in the middle, and shoes at the bottom.
- ☐ Try layered platforms within your cabinets and refrigerator to store items such as canned goods and jars, allowing you to see each item.

Index Card

- ☐ For storage, hole punch a corner in each card, and place them all on a binder ring. You can also place them inside of an index card, often equipped with divider tabs and labels.
- ☐ Write in color to help you visually remember your notes. Adding stickers or drawings that relate to the study topic can also assist.

Miscellaneous

- ☐ Make changes to stress less, but don't stress over what you can't change.
- ☐ Time management is the key to productivity.

Planner

- ☐ Stickers are a great way to spice up your planner, and bring attention to important dates.
- ☐ Worried about losing your page? Most planners come with a bookmark!

School

- ☐ Complete assignments at least one week in advance to make sure you'll never be behind.

Sticky Notes

- Did you know that there is a way to remove a single sticky note from its pad, without it curling up? The key is to remove it from side to side. Lifting from a bottom corner to the top creates a bend, which makes the paper curl.

I challenge you to get creative! What other ways can everyday household items be used to help you get organized? Reach out via the options above to discuss!

Early Life

Tonia M. Monroe was born in Daytona Beach, FL, and is the eldest of two daughters. They were raised in a strict, military inspired household. Enough said, right?!

Education

Tonia graduated from Atlantic High School while simultaneously working towards her Associates of Arts degree from Daytona Beach Community College, now Daytona State College. Due to a huge family argument, Tonia was forced to pay for her final course of her AA, and all of her BAS out of pocket. By August of 2018, she received her Bachelors of Applied Science in Business, with a minor in entrepreneurship, along with a certificate in entrepreneurship from Bethune-Cookman University.

Career

Tonia has held a variety of roles throughout her career path. In chronological order, they are:

Gaming Store Manager > Mall Retail Associate > Bank Teller (PT) and Newborn Hearing Screener (PT) > Bank Teller (FT) > Associate Leader (money lender) > Commercial Lines Processor > Personal Lines Underwriter > Commercial Lines Middle Market Underwriter

During her time as an underwriter is when she began monetizing her organizing skills though Organization And Me, LLC.

Other Work

Tonia has also held the roles of mentor, trainer, and props manager (LJEG).